HUSTLING HOUSES

"I'M STILL HUSTLING, MY PRODUCT IS JUST DIFFERENT!"

For Beginner Real Estate Investors

A Step-By-Step Guide for Flipping Without a Contractor

BY

LESHUN BOYD-GORDON

Hustling Houses

© 2020, One Yes Publishing, LLC

Library of Congress Control Number: 2020946614

The information outlined in this book is for learning purposes only.

This is the intellectual property of One Yes Publishing, LLC. It can't be copied, transmitted or shared and/or published in any form or by any means, electronic, mechanical, photocopying, recording, or otherwise, without the authorization of the author. All rights reserved.

This book is dedicated to my younger self; you never gave up, you always fought back. You never let life push you around; instead, you pushed life around, and for that reason, I am now a stronger man.

I've learned the hard ways to win… This blueprint will provide an easier win for you!

LESHUN BOYD-GORDON

CONTENTS

INTRODUCTION 1

WHEN STARTING YOUR BUSINESS 2

PERMITS REQUIRED FOR FULL GUT JOB (REHAB) 6

THE WORLD OF PERMITS 7

BREAKING DOWN THE PROCESS 14

STAGE 1 | DEMO 20

    STAGE 1 23

    DEMO/CLEANOUT 23

    STAGE 1 25

    REMOVING OLD ROOF-PREP FOR NEW SHINGLE/RUBBER ROOF 25

STAGE 2 | FRAMING 27

STAGE 3 | MECHANICS 30

    STAGE 3 31

    RESIDENTIAL ELECTRICAL STAGE 31

    STAGE 3 32

    PLUMBING 32

    STAGE 3 34

    HVAC ROUGH- IN STAGE 34

STAGE 4 | INSULATION AND DRYWALL 40

    STAGE 4 41

    INSTALLATION DRYWALL 41

    STAGE 4 42

    INSTALLATION DRYWALL 42

STAGE 5 | THE FINISHES 45

    STAGE 5 50

THE FINISHES	50
STAGE 5	51
THE FINISHES	51
STAGE 5	52
THE FINISHES	52
STAGE 5	54
THE FINISHES	54
STAGE 5	56
THE FINISHES	56
APPENDIX SECTION`	**59**
FAQ TO THE AUTHOR	**61**
INVESTOR MOTIVATION	**63**
**ONE YES PUBLISHING	MOTTO**	**64**
INVESTOR ADVICE	**65**
HUSTLING HOUSES	**66**

INTRODUCTION

Hustling Houses is a blueprint designed to guide those who are aspiring real estate investors. It breaks down secrets to "Flipping Without A Contractor." *Hustling Houses* covers a step by step formula used in real estate investing across the world and breaks down the processes of construction rehabilitation one stage at a time.

Even though nothing beats hands-on experience, let this step-by-step guide build your confidence and help you reveal your internal hustler's spirit. Trust me, there is no such thing as an overnight success story. I went broke self-testing and mastering this formula. I know there are many ways to achieve success in the real estate market; however, over the years, I've found this formula works best and produces a smoother outcome and finished project. Chapter by chapter, I will shed light on the failures and successes I encountered on my journey to creating a million-dollar net worth in two and a half years in real estate. This is my way of passing the torch...

Leshun Boyd-Gordon

LET ME REPHRASE

This is flipping without the need of a Contractor, but I didn't say without a Sub-contractor. Both Contractors or subcontractors work on a freelance or contractual basis. Instead, contractors are the bigger picture persons that manage the project and put all the pieces together.

Here, pieces are sub-contractors that are hired by the contractor (general contractor).

To better understand the difference, think of a Contractor as a Teacher that has a substitute. Both are rarely working simultaneously but have a common goal. In which, the teacher has laid out the lesson plan for the substitute.

Translation: The client and Contractor negotiate a deal; however, the subcontractor only negotiates deals with the contractor who has already secured the overall project. This book will replace your need for a contractor, and you're free to hire sub-contractors. Remember, you must provide your Substitute/subcontractor with a lesson plan|Site or building plan. This Plan doesn't have to be a physical copy. Instead, you must be able to articulate your expectations to your subcontractors well enough to be on the same page.

Investors Tip: pay an inspector to do period inspections throughout your rehab, until you are experienced enough.

WHEN STARTING YOUR BUSINESS

So, you want to flip houses? Think you have what it takes to be a real estate investor? Flipping houses requires three key tasks: buying a property, reviving it, and generating a profit when the time comes to sell the property.

House flippers find homes that the average homebuyers are not willing to renovate and develop them to meet specified current market demand. The goal is to introduce the average homebuyer to a property that is move-in ready.

Once you take the steps to fully understand what house flipping is, research if this industry is for you, and if you're ready to jump in, then creating the foundation for your business is the first step.

Create an LLC

An LLC can be formed in most states in a few easy steps. Check out your state guidelines to start the process. Creating a name, choosing a registering agency, filing with the state you plan to do business in and applying for your Employer Identification Number (EIN) through the IRS website are just a few of the key checklist items to getting your LLC ready to do business.

Opening a Bank Account for LLC

Whether to purchase materials for flipping or paying contractors for jobs completed, you must definitely want to set up a business bank account for your LLC. Maintaining a separate bank account will come in handy when dealing with taxes you owe and when working one-on-one with your accountant. As a business owner, it will get far more respect from contractors and trade companies if you directly pay them with a check showing your business name. Also, establishing a personal business relationship with a bank could help you down the road with future investments.

Plan to Finance Your Operation

Before making an offer on a potential investment property, make sure you clearly understand how you plan to fund your operation. Whether self-funded or financed through a lending institution, every aspiring real estate investor need funds to successfully flip houses.

When reviewing pricing on loans for flipping houses, pay close attention to fees. Interest rates will be high on all bridge loans, compared to long-term traditional homeowner mortgages, but they actually matter less. Usually, you'll be making only a handful of payments, so interest rates have less impact on your total house flipping cost than fees do.

Add Funds To Your Bank Account For Your Operating Budget

Once you have business expenses, take the time to transfer money from your personal account into your business account. For audit and tax purposes, you want to make sure that what is considered a business expense is clearly defined for your records. If you plan to pay cash for most expenses, keep good records of receipts for end of the year tax filing.

Find Your Property

Another crucial part of learning how to flip houses is learning how to find good deals. That means not only buying below market value, but within reasonable margins to cover your many expenses: closing costs, material expenses during your rehab project, realtor fees if applicable, and the cost of your efforts and time invested in your operation. Remember, profits are always made in the beginning when you negotiate your purchase price of your investments.

Fix Your Property

As a real estate investor from Day 1, the clock is ticking! Approximately every month that goes by, you will be paying interest and other costs (if applicable): utilities, taxes, insurance, and any other key costs of owning that specific property. All of these things are considered holding costs. To sum it all up, it is money lost! The quicker you can finalize the rehab project, the faster you can flip the property and settle (pay off) your loan or recoup your initial overall investment plus profits. And the quicker you get your payday and move on to the next investment project.

Successfully flipping houses is in several aspects a practice in efficiency. Trust me when I tell you, some contractors will tell you, "Oh sure, we can complete this project in a week flat!" Then four weeks later, they're still trying to line out the electrical plan. Don't be fooled, there's game and finesse in this industry as well. The hustle is the same, except the game and the players are just different, so be mindful.

The same goes for projected price estimates. Too often I have had contractors try to increase the project's price tag on me halfway through a house flip. (Do not allow it!)

All the more reason to select your contractors with much caution. If you've never worked with a specific contractor before, reach out to as many different resources as possible. One

of my methods that I love to do is walk through one of their current projects and see their work myself.

PERMITS REQUIRED FOR FULL GUT JOB
(REHAB)

1| INTERIOR DEMOLITION | CLEAN-OUT | GUT JOB

2| ALTERATIONS

3| MECHANICS | HVAC

4| ELECTRIC

5| PLUMBING

Investor Tip: No matter what type of neighborhood your property may be in, I suggest installing paper blinds to cover all the windows. This prevents people from seeing what you are doing on the inside, especially if you have material in the house. Usually this keeps thieves and vandals from being enticed.

THE WORLD OF PERMITS

This section will outline the wonderful world of permits (Checkout picture of me with my first permit). As a real estate investor, you will need to familiarize yourself with the permit process and how to apply for permits needed to successfully flip houses. Let's take some time to break down five core permits required to professionally perform a full gut job (rehab). Below I will detail for you a full rundown of each specific permit, including a summary of the work connected with each specific Permit.

1| INTERIOR DEMO PERMIT: INTERIOR NON-LOAD BEARING DEMOLITION

An interior demo permit authorizes you to clear out a house of all debris, erect plumbing, interior doors, wiring, drywall, heating/cooling ductwork or radiators and tear down partition walls, also known as non-load bearing walls. Partition walls are usually the walls that divide the bedroom from the bathroom, the walls in the hallway leading to the bedrooms/ and or bathroom, also the wall that separates the living room from the dining room, etc. In general, these walls can be safely taken down without disturbing the overall integrity of a property. Before removing any walls, identify all load-bearing walls because if not supported correctly, you risk causing the entire structure collapsing. Here are a few quick notes on how to identify load-bearing walls in your demo project:

- **Start from the lowest level of the property** (foundation) to determine load vs. non-load-bearing walls. If the house has a basement, then this is the perfect place to begin.

- **Access the original building blueprints** if available for review.

- Call a building inspector or hire a home remodel consultant if you have doubts. **Getting outside help is always an option!**

2| ALTERATIONS BUILDING PERMITS

An alteration permit gives you the authority to make multiple alterations to a building except any structural alterations. These alterations include sheetrock (drywall), doors, flooring, framing, paint, cabinets, windows, siding and stucco. In most states, building permits are required before starting projects to remove, change, repair, add or to install equipment to a structure.

This includes both of the below scenarios:

- New Construction
- Alteration and Additions to Existing Structures.

Total fees are based upon the physical construction area (square footage) or at a percentage (%) of the overall construction costs. Check with your local state government to get familiar with your city's specific ordinances and codes. Be mindful that codes may vary city to city, but the majority of cities across the United States maintain updated documents, ordinances, and codes which are most often readily available on their website.

3| MECHANICS PERMIT

Mechanics permit authorizes you to install ductwork, furnaces and returns with up to 90% better efficiency. Generally, a qualified contractor or licensed HVAC technician (heating, air and conditioning) can request (pull) this mechanical permit for you to begin the process.

This permit allowance includes:

- Ductwork Installations
- Warm Air Equipment
- Warm Air Appliance Installation

4| ELECTRICAL PERMIT

To be approved for an electrical permit, a registered master electrician MUST complete all required documentation submitted in a sealed application along with a copy of current insurance certificates and tax clearance.

Investor Tip: An electrical permit doesn't require the submission of building or site plans.

Electrical inspections: After the roof, framing, fire-stopping, draft-stopping, fire-blocking, and bracing are in place and all electrical wiring is set up (rough-in), a qualified inspector will come perform an electrical rough-in inspection. It's important to note that before any walls or the ceilings are installed, this electrical rough-in inspection is mandatory (required).

** In general, *these outlined steps cater to commercial or residential properties. Strategically, decide which steps you may need to perform because all homes or commercial properties comprise different exterior foundations. Some may consist of brick, metal, wood, or a combination of a few of these materials, so remain mindful when submitting permits.*

5| PLUMBING PERMIT

To receive a plumbing permit, a registered master plumber must submit a completed application. Permits are required for installing, altering, or abandoning a plumbing system without submitting site plans by meeting the conditions and development necessities below.

If the existing structure is not condemned, not required to be brought up to code or a new construction, the homeowner isn't required to have a license to perform normal maintenance repairs on their own home. However, check with your local city's government to see if a homeowner's permit must be pulled or not.

A non-professional site plan must be submitted by the applicant if you are constructing additional patios, carports, decks, porches, swimming pools, or installing structures of 100 square feet or more. Usually, all you have to do is sketch an outline of the construction area, including any setbacks (this doesn't have to be perfect. However, do your best to show proper calculations on any measurements, etc. The zoning staff will review it at that moment and assist if it needs any corrections. You'll receive the permit the same day you apply for the permit.

PERMIT FILING FEES

At the point when plans are submitted as a major aspect of a structural (building) permit application, a documenting expense must be submitted with the application. This none-refundable recording charge will be credited toward the last permit expense.

*A list of processing times and filing fees are available on your city's website.

ADDITIONAL PERMIT REQUIREMENTS

All work must be performed by a licensed Contractor with the accompanying special cases. Work might be performed by an owner living on the premises of a current dwelling or a registered state home improvement contractor, keeping up a State Commercial Activity License.

PERMITS THAT DO NOT REQUIRE THE SUBMISSION OF PLANS

Commercial Window and Door Replacement: A permit is not required for the replacement of a window/door in an existing wall opening.

Electrical Permit: Only a licensed electrical contractor can pull an electrical permit.

Plumbing Permit: Only licensed plumbing contractors can pull a plumbing permit.

Building Permits (May Require a Non-Professional Site Plan Sketch): Building permits are required before beginning projects to enlarge, repair, change or demolish a structure and to install equipment or systems in a structure.

Interior Demolition: If you are completing a demo of all existing interior besides Load-bearing walls.

Re-Roofing Roof: If you are replacing or repairing up to 10% of the existing roofing.

*Please note, these rules are specific to the state of Tennessee. Please check with your local government for specific regulations in your city.

BREAKING DOWN THE PROCESS

BEFORE YOU BEGIN WORK, YOU MUST:

GET PERMITS

Be sure all of these are turned off:

- Water
- Electric
- Gas

STAGE 1| DEMO

- Permit Required
- Demo| gut job|Clean-out
- New Roof
- Level foundation | basement Floor (if needed)

STAGE 2 | FRAMING

- Permit Required
- Framing
- New Windows
- New Stairs

STAGE 3 | MECHANICAL

- 3 Permits Required
- Electric Rough-in
- Plumbing Rough-in
- HVAC Rough-in
- Request Inspection

STAGE 4 | INSULATION & DRYWALL

- Insulate
- Fire block
- Drywall (sheetrock)

STAGE 5 | FINISHES

- Flooring (tile or hardwood)
- Interior doors
- Baseboards and trim
- Paint
- Electric finals
- Plumbing finals
- HVAC finals
- Clean-up

- Request Inspection
- Tags (pass or failed Certification)
- Use and Occupancy

It all started with just watching HGTV. I had a nice piece of change saved up & didn't know what I wanted to do with it.

LESHUN BOYD-GORDON

STAGE 1

DEMO/CLEANOUT

STAGE 1|DEMO

Roof, Interior Demo|Clean-out

(permit required)

Step One| GETTING THE REQUIRED PERMITS

- Request to shut off the water service
- Request to shut off the electric|power service
- Request to shut off the gas service (if applicable)

It's demo time! Start by removing everything from the property that's non-structural, such as furniture, physical fixtures and all debris. Pull out (eliminate) the kitchen cabinets, bathtubs, toilets, interior doors, windows, mud plaster on the walls and ceilings, all the non-structural walls, chimney, plumbing, and electric wires (consult licensed electrician if needed). Drain (empty) the water heaters, oil tanks, and radiators, if located within the property. The best option for removal of junk is to order a dumpster, if you don't have a dump truck. My advice to you (as you continue to grow in this industry) is to consider purchasing a dumpster. Though it can be a little pricey to purchase, overall, it will save you money when completing future projects. To start, you can hire a crew of 5-6 individuals to complete the demo process. It should take approximately 2-3 days to finish the total demo (gutting) of the house.

Investor Tip: To save on time, I generally improve the exterior (siding, stucco, paint, brick) of the property immediately to get rid of all eyesores. This way, I don't have to worry about any additional fines or annoying neighbors. Also, I have a roofer laying down a new shingle (rubber) roof while the Demo process is happening on the inside of the property. Generally, a roof job can take 1 day to complete depending on weather conditions and crew size.

Remember, this blueprint is "Flipping Without A Contractor," which means you will need to be present on the project site more than you desire because you've made the financial decision not to hire a contractor. The on-sight experience will come in handy as you continue to add more flips to your investor portfolio. Please be informed that a qualified Contractor can charge an extra fee on top of the total rehab cost. During my first flip, it cost me nearly $30,000 in additional fees when I utilized Contractor services. It took me starting my second flip to realize I was grossly overcharged (*this doesn't mean it will happen to you*). To be honest, I was extremely upset once I took a closer look and analyzed the cost difference (Contractors vs. Self-Flip), but then I recalled something the OG's told me when I was a young man that "you have to pay, to play." Well, they were right, I sure did pay a heavy price tag, but you don't have to!

Once you begin the demo process, you are well on your way to seeing the rehab project unfold. Congratulations, within a few days, the first stage should be complete!

STAGE 1

DEMO/CLEANOUT

STAGE 1

REMOVING OLD ROOF-PREP FOR NEW SHINGLE/RUBBER ROOF

STAGE 2

FRAMING

Investor Tip: It's essential to hire a contractor who knows the construction standards (building codes) in your state because in certain states, metal studs are required. The material changes; however, the process continues as before. With a realistic plan and a dedicated team, in 2-3 weeks, Stage 1 and 2 ought to be finished.

STAGE 2|FRAMING

Step Two| Start Interior Alterations

(Building Permit Required)

During the framing stage, the layout of the project MUST be determined. As mentioned earlier in this book, partition walls will be designed and built during this stage. Both the ceiling and the perimeter of the house are framed during this stage. If you don't understand the practice of framing, recruit an expert (Qualified Architect) to structure the design of the property. It will benefit your developer (builder) to have plans readily available to work from during this process, so there are no misconceptions of what your physical layout should look like. For example, can you clearly communicate to the developer how many bedrooms and bathrooms you want to have? Will it be structured as an open or closed floor plan? These details are highly critical before you start framing, so you should have a clear vision of what the completed project should look like. What will be the size and locations of the closets? Where will the tub, toilet, vanity, stove, refrigerator, washer and dryer or cabinets be set? Any slight miscommunications about the plans or development could slow your overall progress down by days or even weeks. This is why having a solid floor plan is very important. Your floor plans will have all these details outlined and drawn out for the developer to clearly follow. The framing process usually takes approximately one week, depending on the size of your crew. *Remember, timing is very vital in this industry.* That is why I like to hire a crew with as many guys as possible to knock the job out! Also, do not forget that the framing process includes the basement, new stairs, new windows and exterior doors. Once you complete this stage, seal your house up as soon as possible. For easy access to enter the property, install a lockbox on the exterior door.

Consider Framing Material Needed For Residential:

•2x4 Wood Studs (Existing Construction)

•2x6 Wood Studs (New Construction)

Having a budget and solid plan is truly important. For my first house flip, I had a budget and a plan, but once the project started, I immediately realized I had under-budgeted the flip & my plan was totally off.

LESHUN BOYD-GORDON

STAGE 3|MECHANICS

ELECTRIC, PLUMBING, HVAC

- **Electric:** Permit Required

- **Plumbing**: Permit Required

- **Mechanical**: (HVAC) Permit Required

Your electrician will finish the rough-in and incorporate every electric outlet, switches, and fixtures. Also, smoke detectors are installed through the house. To effectively set any outlets in the best possible areas, the electrician must know the layout of the house. Also, he/she needs to know what kind of fixtures will be used throughout the property.

E.g., Are you installing an electric or gas oven, overhead microwave, dishwasher, waste disposal in sink, radiator, heated water tank or potentially a condenser? The electrician must know if the property will incorporate specific lights, chandeliers and/or ceiling fans. It should take 1-2 days for the Electrical Rough-in work to be finished.

* Often the electrician and plumber may work together but separately to prevent future conflict. In my experience, the plumber and HVAC professionals always are at odds over a space to run their lines. The HVAC systems are placed next. Remember, the HVAC systems are large and inflexible. This stage is complete once the HVAC installation is finished.

Investor Tip: Request for Inspection (Passed or Failed Tag)

STAGE 3

RESIDENTIAL ELECTRICAL STAGE

STAGE 3

PLUMBING

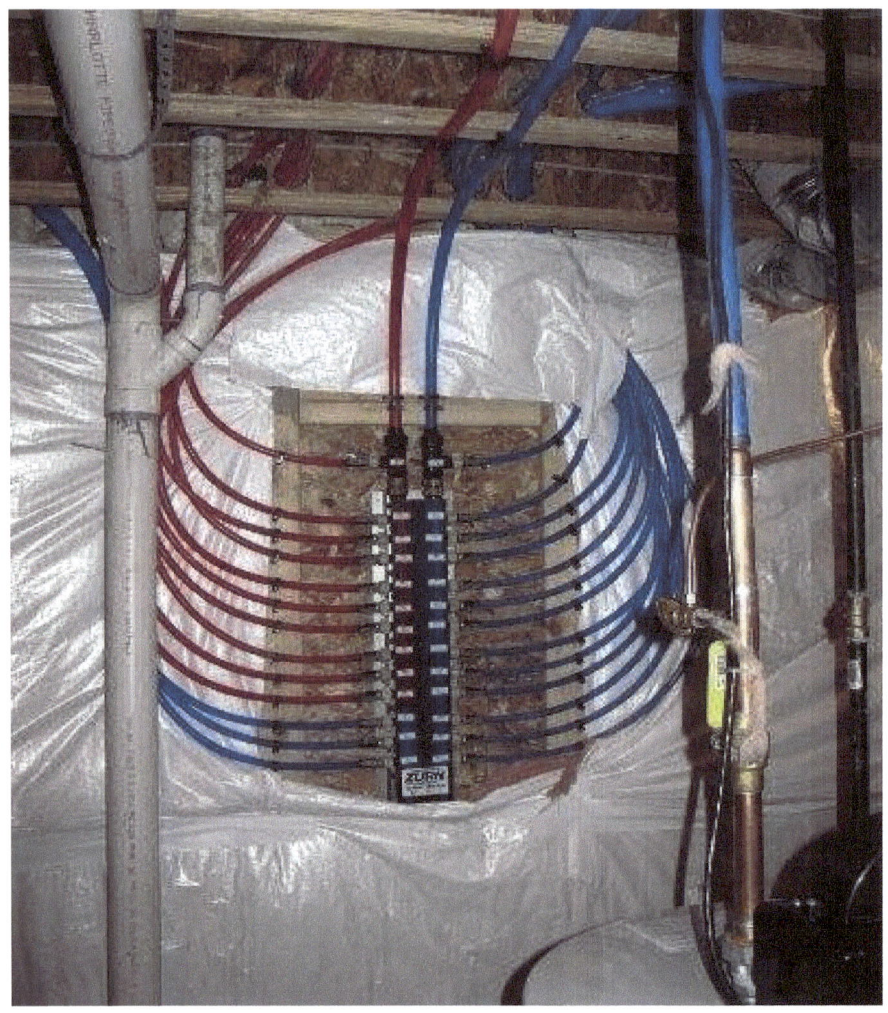

Investor Tip: We use color-coded Red/Blue PEX material that runs directly to a plumbing manifold.

PLUMBING ROUGH- IN PROCESS

If possible, request that the certified plumber begin work with the electrician (time saver method) and to prevent future conflict of material placement. This rough-in process includes the arrangement of a standard bathtub, interior drains, supply lines and a stack pipe that is a vertical pipe that runs from the basement throughout the roof. A stack pipe is made of PVC that removes sewage from a commercial or residential building. The PEX manifold (shown on the last page) is basically like an electric circuit breaker box.

If there's a leak in other bathrooms in the house, you can turn the water supply off to just that bathroom and not interrupt the water flow throughout the rest of the house.

STAGE 3

HVAC ROUGH- IN STAGE

HVAC SYSTEM ADDITION

The final mechanic to be roughed-in is the HVAC system, this is Stage 3. It should take 1-2 days to complete this stage. During the HVAC rough-in, all ductwork and trunks will be installed per the outline layout. Trunks are the passages used in HVAC to deliver and remove air through the system.

Take time to discuss with your HVAC professional the needed airflows for property supply air, return air and exhaust air. I suggest removing or closing off the chimney during the demo stage 1; because once an HVAC system is installed, eventually heat is lost to the outside. Also, you have to worry about steady maintenance, or air-spillage from framing holes. Often, the face of the chimney is kept and upgraded in the finishes stage to bring a modern look to the house. The plumber and HVAC professionals are always at odds over a space to run their lines.

*The plumber has priority because their codes are far stricter.

INSPECTION TIME: ELECTRICAL, PLUMBING AND HVAC

Once the mechanics are complete, it's time to request an inspection from your city's certified inspector. Once scheduled, the city inspector will thoroughly inspect the property framing structure, electrical wiring, plumbing pipeline and the HVAC system.

Investor Tip: The inspector will not proceed with the inspection without checking your previous inspections tags (certifications) to see if they have passed or not. If he/she can't locate them, then your inspector will fail your inspection and write a memo on the back of the certified tag that states something like "previous inspection tags weren't visible or located."

Congratulations: The inspector will give you the final approval to insulate the property once you have passed your inspection. Which means this stage is complete.

Remember to always create relationships while you are handling business. You never know how much money it may save you! Plus, it makes work not feel so much like work.

LESHUN BOYD-GORDON

STAGE 4| INSULATION AND DRYWALL

(INCLUDED WITHIN THE ALTERATIONS PERMIT)

The insulation process can be completed in less than a day. The insulation is added to the wall and ceilings to keep the "heat in" and the "cold out" in the winter months, vice versa for the summer months.

Material:

- **R30 - Ceilings**
- **R19 - Walls** (front and back walls, hallway walls and the basement)

The foam (or fire blocking) will be installed surrounding all interior pipes and wires. If a fire occurred, this would slow down the spread of a fire throughout the property.

STAGE 4

INSTALLATION DRYWALL

Investor Tip: Request For Inspection (Passed or Failed Tag)

You can close up the walls with sheetrock (drywall) once the inspection has passed.

STAGE 4
INSTALLATION DRYWALL

INSTALLATION & DRYWALL

Sheetrock Process, 4 Steps (10) days:

*Make sure outlets, specific wires, switches, recessed lighting, PEX and drains are not completely covered by drywall.

STEP 1: Hanging sheetrock (2) days

*Drywall mud is used to apply the tape to the drywall.

- **Day (1)** Taping (applying first coat of drywall mud)
- **Day (2)** Let tape dry.

STEP 2:

- **Day (3)** Apply the second coat of drywall mud. This coat is thicker to cover the tape, nail holes and any other seams of sheetrock.
- **Day (4, 5)** Let drywall mud dry.

STEP 3:

- **Day (6)** Apply the third and final coat of drywall mud.
- **Day (7, 8)** Let drywall mud dry.

STEP 4:

- **Day (9)** Drywall is sanded down. This process generally takes (2) days to ensure walls and ceilings are one continuous smooth wall.
- **Day (10)** Drywall is sanded down and ready for paint.

I started going to all the home building stores such as Home Depot, Lowe's, etc., & that's how I assembled my first crew. The rest is history...

LESHUN BOYD-GORDON

STAGE 5| THE FINISHES

(INCLUDED WITHIN THE ALTERATIONS PERMIT)

You are almost complete! The finishes stage will take up a lot of time because it's the most detailed part of the entire rehab process. Depending upon your crew size, it could take nearly 3 weeks to finish this stage. The details are the first things everyone will notice when they see the property.

Detail Finishes:

- The paint
- Flooring
- Cabinets
- Light fixtures
- Lay the tile in the basement, bathrooms and kitchen.
- Lay hardwood floors.
- Install baseboards and window and door trim.
- Interior walls, doors, trim and baseboards.
- Hang interior doors, with knobs
- Electric finals, outlet and plug covers, ceiling fans, light fixtures, high hat covers, bathroom ventilation fans, labeling of electric panel, etc.
- Plumbing finals, toilets, vanities, hot water tank, showerheads, faucets, etc.

- HVAC finals, vent covers, furnace and condenser (air conditioning unit)
- Kitchen cabinets, countertop and backsplash with knobs.
- Appliances, refrigerator, stove, mounted microwave and dishwasher.

*All of these are included in the finishes stage.

It's so much value, so many diamonds embedded in our community.

LESHUN BOYD-GORDON

LIVING ROOM REVAMP: BEFORE & AFTER

STAGE 5

THE FINISHES

FINISH LIVING ROOM

STAGE 5

THE FINISHES

FINISHED BEDROOM

STAGE 5

THE FINISHES

FINISHED BATHROOM

STAGE 5

THE FINISHES

FINISHED KITCHEN

FINISHES | EXIT PLAN

Clean the house of any extra material or debris once the finishes are complete. Your electrician, plumber, and HVAC technician will call for an inspection to make sure all codes are met. Each inspector will give you a new electrical, plumbing and HVAC tag (certification). Then you're able to call your city's inspector for your final inspection. All of your permits will be closed out and marked as passed once you've passed your final inspection. After that, you will receive a Use and Occupancy Certification. This is a good time to do any landscaping if you are planning to do so.

Congratulations, your rehab is complete!

STAGE 5

THE FINISHES

FINISHED EXTERIOR OF HOUSE

MESSAGE FROM THE AUTHOR

There are many ways to rehab a house. Depending upon your exit strategy, you should choose rather to do a

"Full Rehab" or "Spruce It Up."

The full rehab of a property will always bring in a higher appraisal than a spruced up project. A full gut job lets the appraiser know that everything incorporated will be new, such as electrical, plumbing, and HVAC. In a sense, a Full Rehab is similar to a new construction project but less expensive. A new construction is when a home is being built from the ground up, which can take approximately 6-8 months. On the other hand, if you decide to carry out a spruce-up project, it'll be much less expensive to do so in comparison to a full gut job. Unfortunately, the appraisal for a spruced-up property will be appraised significantly lower than a full rehab. The spruced-up approach is utilizing as much as you can from the property, such as electrical, plumbing and HVAC. The process consists of simply adding a few upgrades, including new paint, new kitchen and cabinets, bathroom, changing the flooring (new carpet or staining the original hardwood), patching up sheetrock, and maybe even eliminating a partition wall to give the property an open floor plan. All you are doing is glossing up the property. Then you are ready to rent or sell. This process usually takes up to 2-3 weeks.

No matter what approach you decide to take as an investor, all the steps will benefit you and overall save you tens of thousands on your journey to "Flipping Without A Contractor." Remember, all the advice and guidance offered in this book are my opinions and it's other ways to achieve success in this industry. Should you decide to move forward on any of my guidance, please consider doing more research before jumping all in.

Thank you,

LESHUN BOYD-GORDON

APPENDIX SECTION`

FINAL CONSTRUCTION CHECKLIST

- **PERMITS INTERIOR DEMO**

- CLEAN OUT | GUT JOB | DEMO

- ROOF

- CONCRETE BASEMENT - YARD - WHEN NEEDED

- **INSPECTION**

- **ALTERATION BUILDING PERMIT**

- FRAMING

- WINDOWS AND EXTERIOR DOORS

- **ELECTRIC PERMIT**

- ELECTRIC ROUGH-IN

- **PLUMBING PERMIT**

- PLUMBING ROUGH-IN

- **MECHANICAL PERMIT**

- HVAC ROUGH-IN

- **3RD PARTY ELECTRIC CERT**

- INSPECTION

- INSULATION | FIRE-BLOCK

- INSPECTION
- SHEETROCK | TAPE
- FLOORING THROUGHOUT PROPERTY
- INSTALL RAILINGS
- INSTALL ALL INTERIOR DOORS
- PRIME & PAINT; EVERYTHING INCLUDING DOORS
- PLUMBING FINAL
- ELECTRICAL FINAL
- KITCHEN CABINETS, COUNTERTOP & BACKSPLASH FINAL
- CLEANING
- WALK THROUGH WITH OWNER
- **FINAL INSPECTION**
- LIST PROPERTY | RENT PROPERTY

FAQ TO THE AUTHOR

How Did You Get Started In Real Estate?

It all started with just watching HGTV. I had a nice piece of change saved up & didn't know what I wanted to do with it. Over the years, I was always funding my musical career and spent 2013k on promotion and still wasn't as successful as I wanted to be.

A few more episodes later. . . I just jumped, I didn't know anyone. Only the information and influence of HGTV. . . I searched for homes to buy, and I failed a few times, and then I found one that just spoke to me. It made sense to me. Everyone else was against it, but I rolled with it. I started going to all the home building stores such as Home Depot, Lowe's, etc. & that's how I assembled my crew. The rest is history. . . I'm still learning.

What Advice Do You Have For New Real Estate Investors?

Always start with a pest control inspection, then the foundation and work down the list from there. Those first two steps are vital to purchasing and flipping a home because it can be very costly if you skip either.

How Do You Select Your Construction Crews?

Don't listen to crew leaders who say they can do everything! Slowly piece your crews together and follow up with the completion of one job before allowing another job to get started. Consider having more than one crew work simultaneously & do it right the first time! Some crew leaders will try to say you will save money if you run with the "all in one person," but in this game, time is money. Say no, thank you.

How Did I Feel While Doing My First Gut Job (Rehab)?

When I came to the halfway point of completing my first flip project, I was ambushed with so many signs that said my home would be worth $50,000 less than I originally budgeted. Initially, I had my property appraised and was told that my flip would sell around $120,000+ based on market comparable houses. Well, it took me 1 1/2 years to get nearly 50% finished with the flip because *when I started, I didn't have a bucket full of money. I actually had set up a working budget that disappeared quickly once I began the project. Luckily, I had another stream of income producing enough money to allow me to have extra money left over after paying all of my primary bills. I utilized that extra cash by pouring it into my flip. That's why having a budget & plan is truly important.*

INVESTOR MOTIVATION

A seed doesn't need to be watered by the one who plants it, in order for it to grow.

- Leshun Boyd-Gordon

What you don't know, keeps you broke, so learn and know more.

-Leshun Boyd-Gordon

Keep your mind sharp enough to stay on point.

-Leshun Boyd-Gordon

If you think about something long enough, you'll bring it to life.

-Leshun Boyd-Gordon

With a good plan and the right amount of passion, you can conquer most things.

-Leshun Boyd-Gordon

ONE YES PUBLISHING | MOTTO

You will sit in 100 different interviews and you will not get the job. The reality is that you will hear more no's than yes's.

You will fail a lot, I mean a whole lot. But what I ask for you today is to not take No for an answer!

Don't be afraid of No's but be faced with the possibility of missing out on that one Yes you may have prematurely destroyed because all your family & friends have discouraged you along the way.

Welcome the word No!! A good NO prepares you for a grateful Yes! Telling me no is like adding fuel to a fire!

Today, I challenge you to fight back, to work harder & believe in Yourself so heavily that you will not be afraid of the word No, but you will choose to welcome it because you know deep down inside that all it takes is ONE Yes!

INVESTOR ADVICE

Gentrification is literally happening all around you. Go back and buy back! The suburbs will be trash, don't fall for the push out trick.

Think about it... If you were to buy back in your neighborhood | ghetto, it'll be less expensive. In five years or less, the property will be prime real estate depending on its proximity to downtown.

But if you decide to relocate to the suburbs like certain investors intend for you to do, in five years or less, the suburbs will be the refined ghetto!

Do you see the chess game being played before your very eyes? Hopefully, after reading this you can get in the game and score some points.

Please, buy back into your neighborhoods, wait it out and/or if you're still in the ghetto, never leave. Don't sell, at least not yet! Wait it out as long as you can and they'll pay you top dollar to own what you possess.

THE HOODS AND GHETTOS ARE HIDDEN GEMS!

HUSTLING HOUSES

"I'M STILL HUSTLING, MY PRODUCT IS JUST DIFFERENT!"

For Beginner Real Estate Investors

A Step-By-Step Guide for Flipping Without a Contractor

www.ingramcontent.com/pod-product-compliance
Lightning Source LLC
Chambersburg PA
CBHW041832300426
44111CB00002B/64